of light. The intensity of the colours is also the direct result of this method of production. In later centuries transparent enamels came into use, which were laid on to the colourless glass and fired in. If the colours were applied thickly the effect tended to be flat and heavy, whereas the old craftsmen by merely using somewhat thicker panes of glass obtained colours that remained transparent but took on deep and glowing tones.

Unlike the glass-makers the glass-painters always worked in the immediate vicinity of the building. This was essential to avoid the difficulty of transporting the panels and in order to fit them in bulk into the different windows, which were never of a standard size. In Theophilus' time the glass-painter sketched out a design for the panels in their actual size upon a wooden bench covered with chalk. Later artists used parchment or even metal for the purpose. The coloured pieces were laid out on this cartoon and then "cut" with a red-hot iron. Often they had to be cut down to shape still more accurately by means of an iron tool. When all the pieces of mosaic were ready, they were laid out side by side on the cartoon. The features, hands and drapery folds were painted in, with touches of modelling here and there. A browny-black mixture of iron-filings and resin was used for this purpose. Often a ground of this "grisaille" was laid on and parts of it removed with a wooden instrument in order to get high lights. This is how lighter inscriptions were brought out against darker grounds. Finally the grisaille was fired at great heat. The individual pieces of glass were then fastened together with lead, joined up into panels of forty to eighty centimetres, and built into vast compositions by means of an iron framework. Originally all the windows in Chartres were surrounded by great wooden frames which were let into the walls, but these wooden frames were later replaced by iron ones.

The medieval glass-painters were obviously possessed of exquisite taste and extensive experience in the grouping of different colours whose interplay and counteracting influences had to be kept constantly in mind as well as the problem of harmonizing whole areas of colour with the site allotted to the window in the edifice. The lead-lines, reinforced here and there with grisaille, provide the outlines of the design; the network of lead connects the separate pieces and breaks up the strong colours. The composition makes use of one plane only; the windows form one continuous unit with the walls, filling the openings with their colourful tapestries, but never breaking the continuity by using perspective or in any way projecting out.

"What should one do on entering a church?" is one of the questions in an early medieval catechism of the bishopric of Tréguier (Côtes-du-Nord). The answer seems surprising: "Take Holy Water, pray to the Almighty, then wander round the church and look at the stained glass." To appreciate this injunction fully we must go back about eight hundred years. In the whole church there would be no more than a handful of manuscripts, the missal and the psalter, and only the "clerks" were literate. The faithful "read" the stained glass windows. Everything they where supposed to know about the kings and prophets of the Old Testament, about Christ and his Mother, the martyrs and the patron saints, stood there before them, clothed in glorious hues and forms. This was the main purpose behind the coloured windows of the Middle Ages. As Suger, one of the twelfth century abbots of St-Denis, puts it: "The pictures in the windows are primarily for the humble, who cannot read the Word, to show them what they are to believe."

A church interior bathed in cold, clear daylight such as we find today in cathedrals that have lost their original coloured glass would have been unthinkable in the Middle Ages. The gothic architect left bare these great openings in the expanse of wall because he knew the glaziers would come after him and shut out the harsh light, or at least temper it to a twilight atmosphere. The lofty sweep of the gothic vaulting and the elimination of the galleries facilitated en even, homogeneous illumination very different from the stark contrasts of light and shade typical of a romanesque church. Emile Mâle, the well-known French art historian, maintains that from a certain period on, a gothic building can be regarded as the shrine that sets off the stained glass it accommodates. The finest example of this is undoubtedly the Sainte-Chapelle in Paris.

Although these church windows were intended primarily to serve the purpose of lighting the edifice and providing material for instructive contemplation, there can be no doubt of their value as works of decorative art. They harmonize perfectly with the architecture. In its golden age the art of glass-painting could more aptly be compared with that of the imposing masterpieces of romanesque fresco painting, with which it is closely allied, than with the "painting on glass" of later centuries. Although, in the twelfth century especially, the composition of such a window did not go beyond juxtaposing a series of individually worked out details, yet the craftsmen knew how to give to the whole a tonal harmony that made of it a unified work of art. This form of artistic composition reached its highest perfection in the great rose windows of the following century.

The stained glass windows of Chartres can also be considered in connection with their donors, for they constitute a series of votive pictures at the most famous shrine of Our Lady in the medieval western world. The founders include all ranks of society. Kings and nobles, clergy and craftsmen vied with each other to establish the most beautiful window as "an ever-blazing torch" for their beloved church. Their names were seldom recorded. We find their portraits or, in the case of guilds, some small representation of the trade concerned at the bottom of each window. A few of the windows bear the coats of arms of famous families (Pls. IX and XIV).

Four of the most costly windows were taken from an earlier romanesque church destroyed by fire in 1194. They are the survivors of a series of twenty windows donated by the clergy. In the thirteenth century too, a large number of the windows were given by bishops and canons. The splendid rose in the north transept is a gift of the French royal house during the time of Blanca of Castille (Pls. X and XVI). Its counterpart was donated by Pierre Mauclerc, Comte de Dreux (Pls. XVII–XIX). The largest number were, however, presented by the guilds. The windows around the High Altar are from the bakers, butchers, money changers and furriers. Nearly all the storied windows in the ambulatory, the side aisles, and the clerestory are from the guilds. In many of the windows we find realistic representations of the work of the guilds: the cobbler at his last, the weaver at his loom, tradesmen and vintners at their daily tasks. In church the artisan takes his place by the side of the nobleman; the work of his hands is his patent of nobility.

Naturally, only a limited number of the windows can be reproduced in this collection and the choice has been further determined by the technical possibilities of photography and colour-printing. In all, there are a hundred and seventy-three windows in Chartres cathedral. That means a total area of over two thousand square metres of coloured glass. The windows from the early romanesque church are: the middle section of the second lancet window in the south ambulatory, called "Notre Dame de la Belle-Verrière" and the three big windows above the west entrance. These last, "The Tree of Jesse", "The Life of Christ" and "The Passion" are considered some of the most notable examples of French stained glass to be seen anywhere, and certainly rank as the finest in the cathedral (Pls. I–VI). They date from the middle of the twelfth century.

All the coloured windows in the present gothic cathedral were installed between 1200 and 1240. The side aisles, the ambulatory and the encircling chapels contain sixty-eight storied windows, mostly depicting the life of some saint. There are small panels filled with infinitely varying motifs against a background of brillant glass mosaic. The two big roses with their lancets in the gables of the two transepts are among the richest and most beautiful creations of thirteenth century craftsmanship in glass (Pls. X–XIX). The roses show Christ in Glory and the Virgin in Glory. The lancets underneath feature kings and high priests of the Old Testament, prophets and evangelists. The size of the figures and the exceptional brilliance of their attire make a particularly vivid impression on the eye.

The man of the Middle Ages felt proud and exhilarated when he surveyed the exquisite windows he had presented to his church. According to Suger, the Abbot of St-Denis, the alms-box for the upkeep of the church was always well filled. The cathedral chapter saw to the necessary repairs and the safeguarding of valuable works of art. Although restorations were not always successful, all the windows of Chartres did remain in good condition until the end of the seventeenth century. Then came a period of changing mentality and total incomprehension. In countless cathedrals and churches the windows were scrapped as "old Gothic lumber". Even in Chartres eight windows were replaced by plain glass in order to shed more light on the new treasures in the choir, "the Age of Enlightenment thus taking heavy toll" (Van der Meer).

The Revolution desecrated the cathedral and left it in a pitiful condition. Then the turn of events brought fresh appreciation of its merits. During both world wars the windows were removed from Chartres to safety as state property; but now after thorough cleaning and expert restoration they shine again in all their former glory.

PLATE I

THE TREE OF JESSE

Lower part of the right-hand window in the west gable
11 ft. 5 in. × 8 ft. 2 in.

The Tree of Jesse, one of the three windows that have survived from the earlier romanesque church, has been acclaimed as the most beautiful stained glass window in the world, mainly on the grounds of the splendid composition of the whole, the delicate draughtsmanship, so well adapted to the possibilities of the medium, and above all the transcendent beauty of the coloration.

Beneath a lamp and a curtain suspended from an overhanging arch Jesse (Isai) is seen lying upon a couch spread with white linen and a red coverlet. The king wears a blue tunic bordered with gold and a conical cap. Out of his loins springs the smooth trunk of the family tree, the branches of which form graceful arabesques ending in multi-coloured leaf-buds. The kings of Judah are depicted against the blue ground of the centre tract while the prophets who foretold the coming of the Messiah stand in the red sections of the side panels.

The window is a faithful illustration of the text from the prophet Isaiah: "And then shall come forth a rod out of the stem of Jesse, and a branch shall grow out of his roots: And the spirit of the Lord shall rest upon him" (Is. XI, 1–2). The design for the composition probably came from the abbey of St-Denis, during the time of the Abbot Suger. There are innumerable windows based on this theme, some much later in date, but non to rival this one in Chartres.

PLATE II

KING FROM THE TREE OF JESSE

Central figure in the fourth panel of the right-hand window in the west gable. 3 ft. 3 in. × 2 ft. 3 in.

The artist has divided the line of Christ's ancestors into four. Swathed in colourful tunics and mantles, with crowns on their heads, they sit enthroned in the branches of the tree to which they cling with both hands.

"They carry neither sceptre nor banderol", writes Emile Mâle, "nor are they playing the harp as often depicted in later versions. Their sole raison d'être is to act as links in a chain of destiny".

PLATE III

THE ANNUNCIATION

First panel, bottom left in the middle window of the west gable.
4 ft. 3 in. × 3 ft. 3 in.

The window over the main entrance, the biggest and one of the most impressive in the cathedral, recounts the life of Christ from the Annunciation to the Entry into Jerusalem. The storied medallions are alternatively square with red backgrounds or round with deep blue grounds. Exceedingly rich ornamental borders run round each individual picture and round the entire window.

The first picture shows the Angel appearing before Mary with right hand raised and the herald's wand in his left. The Virgin has risen from her seat with a gesture of astonishment.

From the iconographical point of view this Annunciation represents a transitional stage between the archaic versions of the romanesque period, in which Mary is mostly seen seated, and the gothic one of the thirteenth century.

PLATE IV

THE MASSACRE OF THE INNOCENTS

Detail from the middle window in the west gable, fifth row, right-hand panel. 1 ft. × 1 ft. 8 in.

The window "tells" the story of the childhood of Jesus according to the Gospel of St. Luke. Every detail in the description receives an astonishingly full treatment in the design. The realistic Massacre in Bethlehem, spread over two panels, is a striking illustration of the prophecy of Jeremiah: "A voice was heard in Ramah, lamentation and bitter weeping: Rahel weeping for her children" – a young mother bends griefstricken over her dead child.

Even in this small fragment the main colours in the window blend harmoniously.

PLATE V

THE CRUCIFIXION

Detail from the left window in the west gable representing the Passion. Left-hand panel of the middle row. 3 ft. 3 in. × 2 ft. 3 in.

The fourteen medallions of this window depict episodes of the Passion from the Last Supper to Christ's appearance before the disciples at Emmaus after the Resurrection. The Crucifixion is one of the best preserved panels.

The green cross, edged with red, stands outlined against the dark blue sky. Christ is nailed to the tree. He wears a loincloth that reaches below the knee. His head droops on to his right shoulder, his eyes are closed. The wound made by the lance is visible in the suffering flesh. The conception differs markedly from the triumphant Crucifixions of the byzantine and romanesque periods and provides a link with the realism of gothic art.

The expressive attitudes of John on the one side of the cross and Mary on the other reveal their anguish and compassion.

PLATE VI

MARY MAGDALENE
ANNOUNCING THE RESURRECTION
TO THE DISCIPLES

Detail from the left window in the west gable representing the Passion. Second roundel, top left. 3 ft. 3 in. × 2 ft. 3 in.

The roundels of the Passion window are among the most beautiful glass-paintings of the twelfth century. Their simple design is admirably adapted to the peculiar limitations and potentialities of glass mosaic. Rich primary colours have been so combined as to ensure the general effect of harmony.

Mary Magdalene has found Christ's grave empty and learned from the Angel of His resurrection. She conveys these tidings to three disciples who raise their hands in astonishment and wonder at the news. Iconography teaches us that the first of the three disciples is Peter.

PLATE VII

ROUNDEL FROM THE
CHARLEMAGNE WINDOW

Middle roundel of the second window to the left of the central apsidal chapel in the ambulatory. Diameter 2 ft. 8 in.

One of the best preserved and brightest storied windows in the ambulatory relates the history of Charlemagne. Twenty-two pictures are devoted to the account of his military exploits in the East, the wars against the Saracens in Spain, and the most important incidents in the Song of Roland.

This roundel depicts an episode from the second of these cycles. In answer to a command from St. James, Charlemagne has just taken the city of Pamplona. He is here seen on horseback instructing the masons engaged in building a church to be dedicated to St. James.

The storied windows are among the most astounding achievements in stained glass technique. As many as four hundred pieces of glass may be used to the square metre, all linked by lead lines and assembled into pictures which can nevertheless be clearly distinguished, thanks to the simplicity of the design and the dazzling colour contrasts.

PLATE VIII

ST. DENIS HANDING OVER
THE ORIFLAMME

Second window in the clerestory of the east wall in the south transept.
13 ft. 2 in. × 6 ft. 7 in.

The two figures in this window are not merely standing
side by side as are those in the neighbouring ones. They are
performing a rite.

On the left stands St. Denis, dressed in episcopal regalia.
He holds a book in one hand and with the other entrusts
the oriflamme to a knight clad in early thirteenth century
battle dress: chain mail and tunic, with the sword thrust
into a loose girdle. The tunic bears a silver anchor-shaped
cross on an azure field with a red "cost" or cross-band,
the arms of the house of Clément. The knight thus depicted
is presumably Jean Clément, Lord Marshal of Metz and
Argentan, and brother of the Abbot of St-Denis at the
time. The window was probably donated after some campaign
in which the knight had the honour of carrying the oriflamme.

It is thus an historical monument as well as being one
of the show pieces of stained glass.

PLATE IX

DONOR-PANEL SHOWING
KNIGHT-AT-ARMS

Second window in the clerestory of the east wall in the north transept.
Diameter 5 ft. 3 in.

The cathedral windows in Chartres can also be regarded as a series of imposing votive pictures attaching to a famous shrine. The donors were bishops and church dignitaries, kings and nobles, knights and men-at-arms, but mainly guilds. The donors are seldom mentioned by name, but are often recorded for posterity by incorporating into the design of the window either their armorial bearings or some scene from the exercise of their craft or trade.

The donor-panel in the St-Eustace window shows a knight in full armour. His shield has "gyrons" or gores of red and white with a blue fillet and points. The same device is repeated twice in the horse's caparison. This window was probably given by some knight of the house of Beaumont-sur-Oise.

Under Eastern influence there arose round 1220 A.D. the custom of covering the charger with a metal cuirass, which usually bore the arms of the rider. This is the only window displaying a caparison of this type.

PLATE X

"ROSE DE FRANCE"

In the gable of the north transept : Diameter of the rose : 13 m,
the lancet windows : 24 ft. 3 in. × 5 ft. 3 in.

The rose and the five lancet windows were given by the French royal family during the reign of Blanca of Castille, when the cathedral was being built.

The structure of the rose window demonstrates the skill of the masons as well as of the glass-painters. Roundels and quarries are combined in a superb composition. The light from the five soaring lancets falls in solid beams into the dim interior, and the side lights connect the rose and the lancets into a concordant whole.

The rose is dedicated to the Virgin. She sits enthroned in the central medallion surrounded by the Gifts of the Spirit, a circle of angels, the kings of Judah, and the twelve minor prophets. In the centre lancet St-Anne appears with Mary in her arms. Her companions on either side are four of the most famous figures of the Old Testament: David and Solomon, symbolizing the Messiah's royal blood, Melchizedek and Aaron signifying His priesthood.

The arms of the donor, golden lilies on an azure field, can be found among the small quarries in the rose and in the middle lancet.

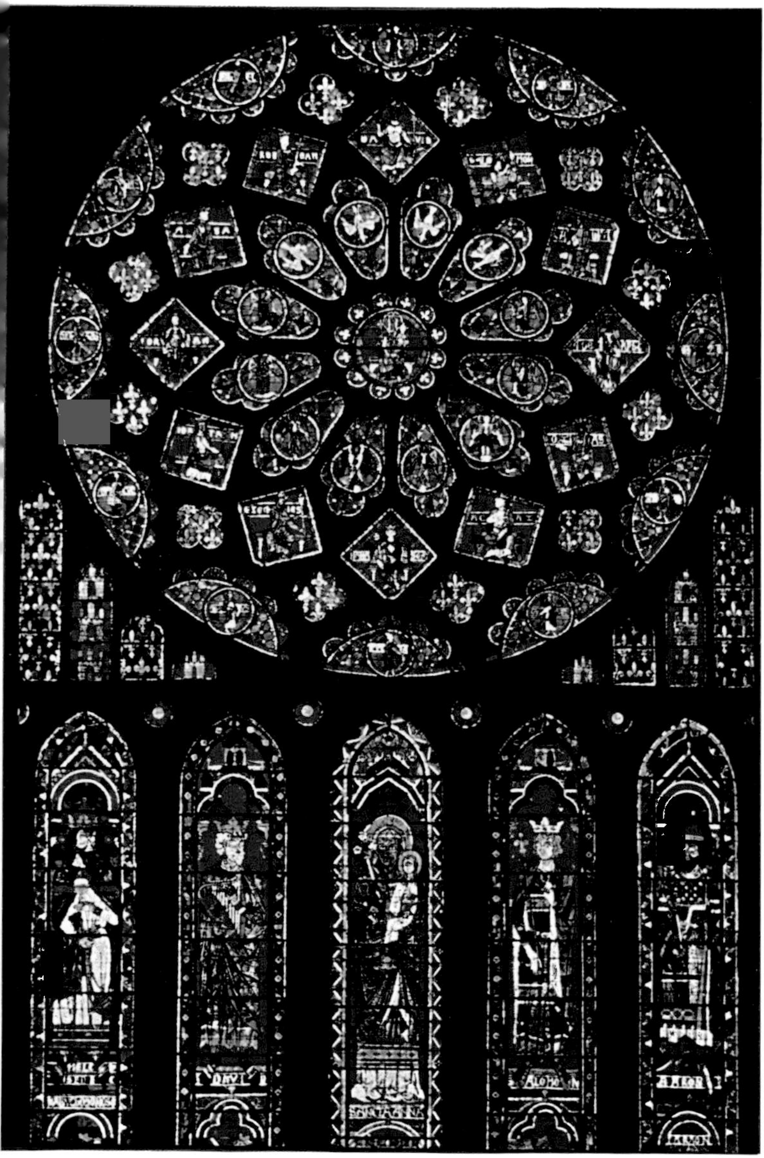

PLATE XI

KING DAVID

Second lancet from the left in the gable of the north transept.
6 ft. 3 in. × 3 ft. 11 in.

The five great figures in the lancets under the "Rose de France" are among the most important work in Chartres cathedral and can be numbered among the more impressive examples of glass painting in general. The two outer ones are set against blue backgrounds, the three inner ones against deep red.

From this glowing red ground the figure of David emerges limned in powerful strokes. He is portrayed as both king and psalmist: he is singing and accompanying himself on the harp. His emerald green mantle is picked out luminously against the red ground, and made to contrast with the blue and yellow introduced in the instrument and mantle-lining.

To reproduce flesh-tints was particularly hard for the medieval glass-painter. As the glass was ready-made in the different colours and colour was not laid on until later, they had the greatest difficulty in finding a flesh tone that approximated to a facial complexion. They often had to be satisfied with pale lilac or a brownish tinge. A further problem lay in the opacity of the red glass. Red and white materials had therefore to be mixed when producing it, hence the white veining visible in the red background.

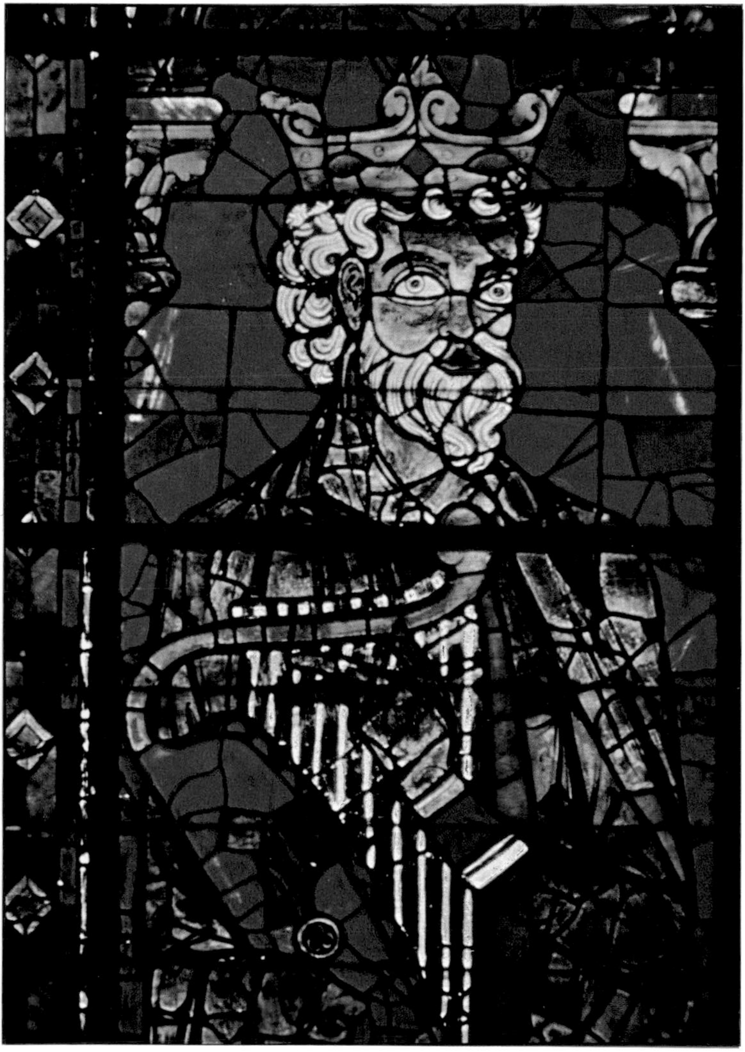

PLATE XII

KING SOLOMON

Second lancet from the right in the gable of the north transept.
8 ft. 2 in. × 4 ft. 11 in.

Enormous size, reposeful lines and rich tonal harmonies, all contribute to make this a majestic figure.

King Solomon is seen in the guise of a young French prince. Crown and sceptre are the symbols of his rank. Locks of hair fall about his face in the fashion prevailing among princes during the late Middle Ages. To let the left hand play with the golden neck-chain seems to have been a favorite trick with French princes, or at least to have been a conventional pose in portraiture. It appears in a whole series of stained glass portraits and also on the famous royal tombs in the abbey-church of St-Denis. Solomon is wearing white gloves and his pale blue mantle is lined with ermine.

The attributes have led many to suppose that this figure is meant to be St-Louis. The window was, in actual fact, installed in Louis IX's early youth, during the regency of his mother Blanca of Castille.

PLATE XIII

AARON THE HIGH PRIEST

First window on the right in the gable of the north transept.
5 ft. 11 in. × 4 ft. 3 in.

Aaron the High Priest here appears robed in all the insignia of office. His left hand clasps the Book of the Law, his right the rod that blossomed and broke into leaf. In designing the vestments the artist has followed the description given in the Second Book of Moses, Chapter 28. The High Priest wears a white tunic and a lilac ephod, with a breast plate studded with twelve precious stones. A great onyx can be seen on the left shoulder. Each of the two clasps fastening the garment is set with stones. A turban with a gold fillet completes the official robes.

In the Catholic Church the flowering rod of Aaron is traditionally interpreted as a symbol of the virgin motherhood of Mary.

PLATE XIV

ARMS OF THE FRENCH
ROYAL HOUSE

Base panel of the central lancet in the gable of the north transept.
5 ft. 7 in. × 5 ft. 7 in.

We find this magnificent escutcheon with its golden lilies on an azure field in the lowest panel of the central lancet under the "Rose de France". The blue and gold form a perfect triad with the flaming red background.

In the smaller lights between the rose and the lancet windows this same blazon alternates with that of the house of Castille, therefore this section must have been executed in the reign of Blanca of Castille (1223–1236).

PLATE XV

THE DEATH OF KING SAUL

Base panel of the second lancet from the left in the gable of the north transept. 5 ft. 11 in. × 3 ft. 11 in.

It is a characteristic feature in thirteenth century religious iconography that the image of a saint or of a great Old Testament figure quite often has some enemy of the Church or some sinner as a tail-piece. Thus we find in the southern porch the effigy of Peter supported by a foot-stool on which Simon the Sorceror is depicted while the figure of St-Andrew stands on the shoulders of the tyrant who put him to death.

This is how we should interpret the conjunction of the massive figure of King David in the lancet under the "Rose de France" with that of Saul beneath him, Saul who had tried to kill David but who instead ended his own life by falling upon his sword after the defeat at Gilboa.

The picture is artless and eloquent in execution. The lustrous blues and reds are keyed in the colour harmony that distinguishes the windows of Chartres, especially the "Rose de France".

PLATE XVI

PHARAOH DROWNING
IN THE RED SEA

Base panel of the right-hand lancet in the gable of the north transept.
4 ft. 11 in. × 4 ft. 3 in.

Under the gigantic figure of Aaron the Priest (Pl. XIII) we see his enemy, the Egyptian Pharaoh, who was engulfed in the waters of the Red Sea while trying to prevent the Jews from reaching the Promised Land.

Within the small compass of this panel, a truly expert hand has succeeded in indicating the calamity by means of one highly stylized symbolic figure. The white horse has planted his four hooves firmly together and his head is bowed to his knees. Without losing the crown from his head and with his spurs still at his heels, Pharaoh tumbles headlong to the ground, while the skirts of his mantle are caught by the waves closing over him.

PLATE XVII

MARK THE EVANGELIST
ON THE SHOULDERS
OF THE PROPHET DANIEL

First lancet on the right in the gable of the south transept.
8 ft. 6 in. × 5 ft. 3 in.

The five lancet windows and the medallions in the great rose of the south transept are among the best preserved glass in the cathedral. In the central lancet window we find a towering figure of Mary. The four compositions to the left and right are particularly interesting for the iconographist. The four great prophets are seen standing upright, each one bearing upon his shoulders one of the four Evangelists. This original conception of the continuity between the Old and New Testaments seems to derive from Rome and is also to be seen in the sculptures of the Bamberger Dom.

The draughtsmanship is astonishingly elegant for the period and the artist has caught the posture of the bearers and of their burdens admirably. The fusion of colours in all these lancets is quite exceptional in character.

PLATE XVIII

YOLANDE DE BRETAGNE

Donor-panel below the left-hand lancet in the gable of the south transept. 3 ft. 11 in. × 5 ft. 3 in.

The glass in the rose and the lancet windows in the gable of the south transept was donated about 1220 by the Comte de Dreux, Pierre Mauclerc and his wife Alix de Bretagne. Their arms of gold and azure chequé with an ermine quarter are to be found in the twelve quarries of the great rose and in the middle lancet beneath.

The artist has deliberately surrounded the members of this illustrious family with the colours of their house and by doing so has drawn the bases of these five lancets together into one decorative unit.

The daughter of the Comte de Dreux, Yolande de Bretagne, stretches up her hands to the immense figure of Mary in the central window. The play of light in the blue background and the use of the bursting leaf-buds as symbolic and ornamental motifs merit particular attention.

PLATE XIX

ALIX DE THOUARS,
COMTESSE DE DREUX

Donor-panel below the 2nd lancet in the gable of the south transept.
5 ft. 3 in. × 3 ft. 11 in.

As in the previous panel, the arms of the Dreux-Bretagne family are repeated in the colours of the countess' robe. The ermine quarter from the escutcheon is worked into the fillet hanging from her right shoulder and the gold and azure chess-board motif appears in her dress. The olive green of the loose-hanging mantle, the typical headdress, the unity of the composition and the reposeful adjustment of the colours are further points to be noticed.

The countess kneels before the huge image of the Virgin in the central lancet, one of the many effigies of the "Lady of Chartres".

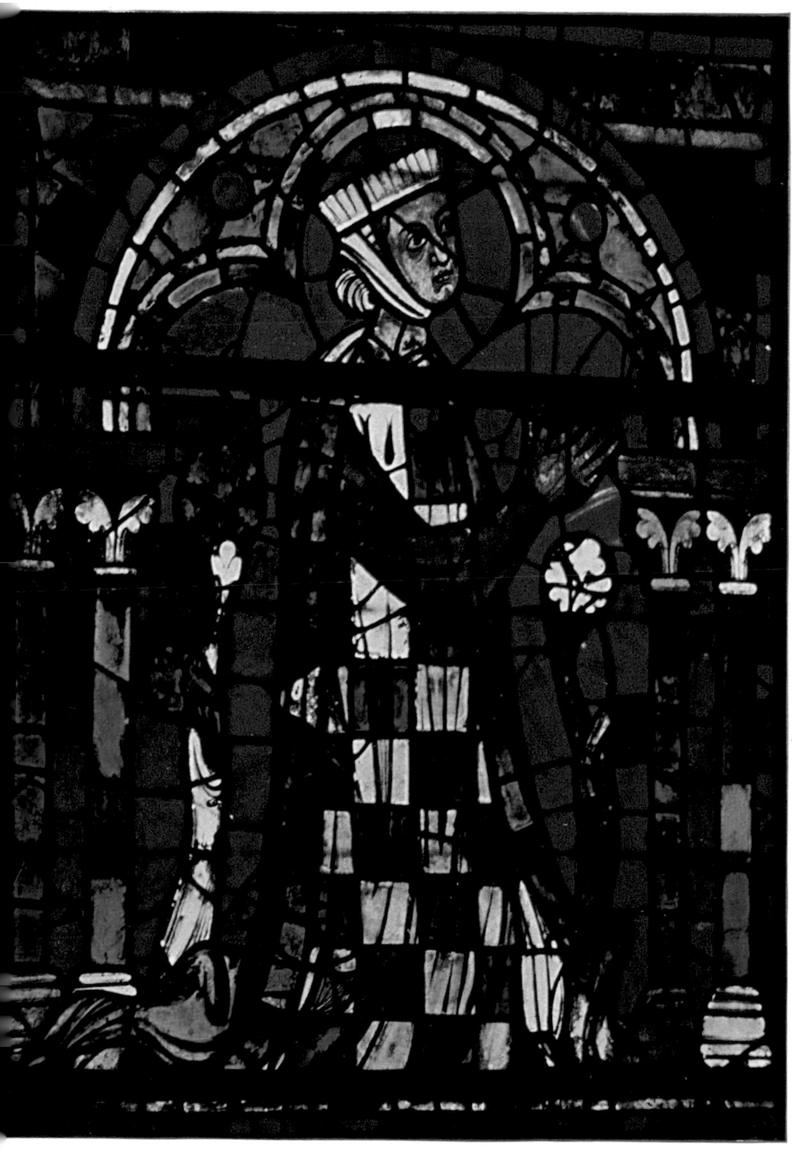

The stained glass windows were photographed by kind permission of the Bishop of Chartres, Son Excellence Monseigneur Harscouet, and the Chief Architect of the Eure-et-Loir Department, Monsieur Jean Maunoury.

The author used an optical instrument specially designed for the purpose and developed the negatives in Chartres by means of a process perfected in the laboratories of the Technical High School of St-Lieven in Ghent.

ORBIS-PICTUS